HOMESCHOOL PLANNER AND RECORD BOOK FOR TEACHERS

LESSON PLAN ORGANIZER NOTEBOOK WITH STUDENT ATTENDANCE TRACKER AND REPORT CARD

KYLIE TAYLOR

This book belongs to:

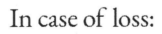

In case of loss:

CURRICULUM PLANNER

AUGUST	SEPTEMBER	OCTOBER	NOVEMBER

DECEMBER	JANUARY	FEBRUARY	MARCH

APRIL	MAY	JUNE	JULY

MONTHLY REMINDERS

MON	TUES	WED	THUR	FRI	SAT

WEEKLY
LESSON OUTLINE

WEEK OF: _____   FROM: _____   TO: _____

MONDAY

TUESDAY

WEDNESDAY

THURSDAY

FRIDAY

SATURDAY

WEEKLY
LESSON OUTLINE

WEEK OF: _____   **FROM:** _____   **TO:** _____

MONDAY	TUESDAY	WEDNESDAY

THURSDAY	FRIDAY	SATURDAY

WEEKLY
LESSON OUTLINE

WEEK OF: _____   FROM: _____   TO: _____

MONDAY	TUESDAY	WEDNESDAY

THURSDAY	FRIDAY	SATURDAY

WEEKLY
LESSON OUTLINE

WEEK OF: _____ **FROM:** _____ **TO:** _____

MONDAY	TUESDAY	WEDNESDAY

THURSDAY	FRIDAY	SATURDAY

ASSIGNMENT/PROJECT RECORD

MONTH: _____   **YEAR:** _____

TASK	DESCRIPTION	GIVEN	DUE	SUBMITTED BY

NOTES

TO DO LIST

MONTHLY REMINDERS

MON	TUES	WED	THUR	FRI	SAT

WEEKLY
LESSON OUTLINE

WEEK OF: _____ **FROM:** _____ **TO:** _____

MONDAY	TUESDAY	WEDNESDAY

THURSDAY	FRIDAY	SATURDAY

WEEKLY LESSON OUTLINE

WEEK OF: _____ FROM: _____ TO: _____

MONDAY	TUESDAY	WEDNESDAY

THURSDAY	FRIDAY	SATURDAY

WEEKLY
LESSON OUTLINE

WEEK OF: _____ **FROM:** _____ **TO:** _____

MONDAY	TUESDAY	WEDNESDAY

THURSDAY	FRIDAY	SATURDAY

WEEKLY LESSON OUTLINE

WEEK OF: _____   FROM: _____   TO: _____

MONDAY	TUESDAY	WEDNESDAY

THURSDAY	FRIDAY	SATURDAY

ASSIGNMENT/PROJECT RECORD

MONTH: _____   **YEAR:** _____

TASK	DESCRIPTION	GIVEN	DUE	SUBMITTED BY

NOTES

TO DO LIST

MONTHLY REMINDERS

MON	TUES	WED	THUR	FRI	SAT

WEEKLY
LESSON OUTLINE

WEEK OF: _____   **FROM:** _____   **TO:** _____

MONDAY	TUESDAY	WEDNESDAY

THURSDAY	FRIDAY	SATURDAY

WEEKLY LESSON OUTLINE

WEEK OF: _____ FROM: _____ TO: _____

MONDAY	TUESDAY	WEDNESDAY

THURSDAY	FRIDAY	SATURDAY

WEEKLY
LESSON OUTLINE

WEEK OF: _____   **FROM:** _____   **TO:** _____

MONDAY	TUESDAY	WEDNESDAY

THURSDAY	FRIDAY	SATURDAY

WEEKLY
LESSON OUTLINE

WEEK OF: _____ **FROM:** _____ **TO:** _____

MONDAY	TUESDAY	WEDNESDAY

THURSDAY	FRIDAY	SATURDAY

ASSIGNMENT/PROJECT RECORD

MONTH: _____   **YEAR:** _____

TASK	DESCRIPTION	GIVEN	DUE	SUBMITTED BY

NOTES

TO DO LIST

MONTHLY REMINDERS

MON	TUES	WED	THUR	FRI	SAT

WEEKLY LESSON OUTLINE

WEEK OF: _____ **FROM:** _____ **TO:** _____

MONDAY	TUESDAY	WEDNESDAY

THURSDAY	FRIDAY	SATURDAY

WEEKLY LESSON OUTLINE

WEEK OF: _____ **FROM:** _____ **TO:** _____

MONDAY	TUESDAY	WEDNESDAY

THURSDAY	FRIDAY	SATURDAY

WEEKLY
LESSON OUTLINE

WEEK OF: _____ **FROM:** _____ **TO:** _____

MONDAY	TUESDAY	WEDNESDAY

THURSDAY	FRIDAY	SATURDAY

WEEKLY LESSON OUTLINE

WEEK OF: _____   FROM: _____   TO: _____

MONDAY	TUESDAY	WEDNESDAY

THURSDAY	FRIDAY	SATURDAY

ASSIGNMENT/PROJECT RECORD

MONTH: _____   **YEAR:** _____

TASK	DESCRIPTION	GIVEN	DUE	SUBMITTED BY

NOTES

TO DO LIST

MONTHLY REMINDERS

MON	TUES	WED	THUR	FRI	SAT

WEEKLY
LESSON OUTLINE

WEEK OF: _____   FROM: _____   TO: _____

MONDAY	TUESDAY	WEDNESDAY

THURSDAY	FRIDAY	SATURDAY

WEEKLY
LESSON OUTLINE

WEEK OF: _____ **FROM:** _____ **TO:** _____

MONDAY	TUESDAY	WEDNESDAY

THURSDAY	FRIDAY	SATURDAY

WEEKLY LESSON OUTLINE

WEEK OF: _____   **FROM:** _____   **TO:** _____

MONDAY

TUESDAY

WEDNESDAY

THURSDAY

FRIDAY

SATURDAY

WEEKLY
LESSON OUTLINE

WEEK OF: _____ **FROM:** _____ **TO:** _____

MONDAY

TUESDAY

WEDNESDAY

THURSDAY

FRIDAY

SATURDAY

ASSIGNMENT/PROJECT RECORD

MONTH: _____ **YEAR:** _____

TASK	DESCRIPTION	GIVEN	DUE	SUBMITTED BY

NOTES

TO DO LIST

MONTHLY REMINDERS

MON	TUES	WED	THUR	FRI	SAT

WEEKLY LESSON OUTLINE

WEEK OF: _____   FROM: _____   TO: _____

MONDAY	TUESDAY	WEDNESDAY

THURSDAY	FRIDAY	SATURDAY

WEEKLY
LESSON OUTLINE

WEEK OF: _____   **FROM:** _____   **TO:** _____

MONDAY	TUESDAY	WEDNESDAY

THURSDAY	FRIDAY	SATURDAY

WEEKLY
LESSON OUTLINE

WEEK OF: _____ **FROM:** _____ **TO:** _____

MONDAY	TUESDAY	WEDNESDAY

THURSDAY	FRIDAY	SATURDAY

WEEKLY LESSON OUTLINE

WEEK OF: _____ **FROM:** _____ **TO:** _____

MONDAY	TUESDAY	WEDNESDAY

THURSDAY	FRIDAY	SATURDAY

ASSIGNMENT/PROJECT RECORD

MONTH: _____   **YEAR:** _____

TASK	DESCRIPTION	GIVEN	DUE	SUBMITTED BY

NOTES

TO DO LIST

MONTHLY REMINDERS

MON	TUES	WED	THUR	FRI	SAT

WEEKLY
LESSON OUTLINE

WEEK OF: _____ **FROM:** _____ **TO:** _____

MONDAY	TUESDAY	WEDNESDAY

THURSDAY	FRIDAY	SATURDAY

WEEKLY
LESSON OUTLINE

WEEK OF: _____ **FROM:** _____ **TO:** _____

MONDAY	TUESDAY	WEDNESDAY

THURSDAY	FRIDAY	SATURDAY

WEEKLY
LESSON OUTLINE

WEEK OF: _____ **FROM:** _____ **TO:** _____

MONDAY	TUESDAY	WEDNESDAY

THURSDAY	FRIDAY	SATURDAY

WEEKLY LESSON OUTLINE

WEEK OF: _____ **FROM:** _____ **TO:** _____

MONDAY	TUESDAY	WEDNESDAY

THURSDAY	FRIDAY	SATURDAY

ASSIGNMENT/PROJECT RECORD

MONTH: _____   **YEAR:** _____

TASK	DESCRIPTION	GIVEN	DUE	SUBMITTED BY

NOTES

TO DO LIST

MONTHLY REMINDERS

MON	TUES	WED	THUR	FRI	SAT

WEEKLY LESSON OUTLINE

WEEK OF: _____ **FROM:** _____ **TO:** _____

MONDAY	TUESDAY	WEDNESDAY

THURSDAY	FRIDAY	SATURDAY

WEEKLY LESSON OUTLINE

WEEK OF: _____ FROM: _____ TO: _____

MONDAY	TUESDAY	WEDNESDAY

THURSDAY	FRIDAY	SATURDAY

WEEKLY
LESSON OUTLINE

WEEK OF: _____ **FROM:** _____ **TO:** _____

MONDAY	TUESDAY	WEDNESDAY

THURSDAY	FRIDAY	SATURDAY

WEEKLY
LESSON OUTLINE

WEEK OF: _____ **FROM:** _____ **TO:** _____

MONDAY	TUESDAY	WEDNESDAY

THURSDAY	FRIDAY	SATURDAY

ASSIGNMENT/PROJECT RECORD

MONTH: _____   **YEAR:** _____

TASK	DESCRIPTION	GIVEN	DUE	SUBMITTED BY

NOTES

TO DO LIST

MONTHLY REMINDERS

MON	TUES	WED	THUR	FRI	SAT

WEEKLY
LESSON OUTLINE

WEEK OF: _____ **FROM:** _____ **TO:** _____

MONDAY	TUESDAY	WEDNESDAY

THURSDAY	FRIDAY	SATURDAY

WEEKLY
LESSON OUTLINE

WEEK OF: _____ **FROM:** _____ **TO:** _____

MONDAY

TUESDAY

WEDNESDAY

THURSDAY

FRIDAY

SATURDAY

WEEKLY
LESSON OUTLINE

WEEK OF: _____ **FROM:** _____ **TO:** _____

MONDAY	TUESDAY	WEDNESDAY

THURSDAY	FRIDAY	SATURDAY

WEEKLY
LESSON OUTLINE

WEEK OF: _____ **FROM:** _____ **TO:** _____

MONDAY	TUESDAY	WEDNESDAY

THURSDAY	FRIDAY	SATURDAY

ASSIGNMENT/PROJECT RECORD

MONTH: _____   **YEAR:** _____

TASK	DESCRIPTION	GIVEN	DUE	SUBMITTED BY

NOTES

TO DO LIST

MONTHLY REMINDERS

MON	TUES	WED	THUR	FRI	SAT

WEEKLY LESSON OUTLINE

WEEK OF: _____ **FROM:** _____ **TO:** _____

MONDAY	TUESDAY	WEDNESDAY

THURSDAY	FRIDAY	SATURDAY

WEEKLY
LESSON OUTLINE

WEEK OF: _____   **FROM:** _____   **TO:** _____

MONDAY	TUESDAY	WEDNESDAY

THURSDAY	FRIDAY	SATURDAY

WEEKLY
LESSON OUTLINE

WEEK OF: _____   **FROM:** _____   **TO:** _____

MONDAY	TUESDAY	WEDNESDAY

THURSDAY	FRIDAY	SATURDAY

WEEKLY
LESSON OUTLINE

WEEK OF: _____ **FROM:** _____ **TO:** _____

MONDAY

TUESDAY

WEDNESDAY

THURSDAY

FRIDAY

SATURDAY

ASSIGNMENT/PROJECT RECORD

MONTH: _____   **YEAR:** _____

TASK	DESCRIPTION	GIVEN	DUE	SUBMITTED BY

NOTES

TO DO LIST

MONTHLY REMINDERS

MON	TUES	WED	THUR	FRI	SAT

WEEKLY
LESSON OUTLINE

WEEK OF: _____ **FROM:** _____ **TO:** _____

MONDAY	TUESDAY	WEDNESDAY

THURSDAY	FRIDAY	SATURDAY

WEEKLY LESSON OUTLINE

WEEK OF: _____ **FROM:** _____ **TO:** _____

MONDAY	TUESDAY	WEDNESDAY

THURSDAY	FRIDAY	SATURDAY

WEEKLY
LESSON OUTLINE

WEEK OF: _____ **FROM:** _____ **TO:** _____

MONDAY

TUESDAY

WEDNESDAY

THURSDAY

FRIDAY

SATURDAY

WEEKLY LESSON OUTLINE

WEEK OF: _____ **FROM:** _____ **TO:** _____

MONDAY

TUESDAY

WEDNESDAY

THURSDAY

FRIDAY

SATURDAY

ASSIGNMENT/PROJECT RECORD

MONTH: _____   **YEAR:** _____

TASK	DESCRIPTION	GIVEN	DUE	SUBMITTED BY

NOTES

TO DO LIST

MONTHLY REMINDERS

MON	TUES	WED	THUR	FRI	SAT

WEEKLY
LESSON OUTLINE

WEEK OF: _____   **FROM:** _____   **TO:** _____

MONDAY

TUESDAY

WEDNESDAY

THURSDAY

FRIDAY

SATURDAY

WEEKLY LESSON OUTLINE

WEEK OF: _____ **FROM:** _____ **TO:** _____

MONDAY	TUESDAY	WEDNESDAY

THURSDAY	FRIDAY	SATURDAY

WEEKLY LESSON OUTLINE

WEEK OF: _____ FROM: _____ TO: _____

MONDAY	TUESDAY	WEDNESDAY

THURSDAY	FRIDAY	SATURDAY

WEEKLY
LESSON OUTLINE

WEEK OF: _____ **FROM:** _____ **TO:** _____

MONDAY	TUESDAY	WEDNESDAY

THURSDAY	FRIDAY	SATURDAY

ASSIGNMENT/PROJECT RECORD

MONTH: _____   **YEAR:** _____

TASK	DESCRIPTION	GIVEN	DUE	SUBMITTED BY

NOTES

TO DO LIST

MONTHLY REMINDERS

MON	TUES	WED	THUR	FRI	SAT

WEEKLY
LESSON OUTLINE

WEEK OF: _____ **FROM:** _____ **TO:** _____

MONDAY	TUESDAY	WEDNESDAY

THURSDAY	FRIDAY	SATURDAY

WEEKLY LESSON OUTLINE

WEEK OF: _____ **FROM:** _____ **TO:** _____

MONDAY	TUESDAY	WEDNESDAY

THURSDAY	FRIDAY	SATURDAY

WEEKLY
LESSON OUTLINE

WEEK OF: _____   FROM: _____   TO: _____

MONDAY	TUESDAY	WEDNESDAY

THURSDAY	FRIDAY	SATURDAY

WEEKLY LESSON OUTLINE

WEEK OF: _____ **FROM:** _____ **TO:** _____

MONDAY	TUESDAY	WEDNESDAY

THURSDAY	FRIDAY	SATURDAY

ASSIGNMENT/PROJECT RECORD

MONTH: _____ **YEAR:** _____

TASK	DESCRIPTION	GIVEN	DUE	SUBMITTED BY

NOTES

TO DO LIST

STUDENT ATTENDANCE TRACKER

NAME OF STUDENT: _____

	AUG	SEPT	OCT	NOV	DEC	JAN	FEB	MAR	APR	MAY	JUNE	JULY
1												
2												
3												
4												
5												
6												
7												
8												
9												
10												
11												
12												
13												
14												
15												
16												
17												
18												
19												
20												
21												
22												
23												
24												
25												
26												
27												
28												
29												
30												
31												

STUDENT ATTENDANCE TRACKER

NAME OF STUDENT: _____

	AUG	SEPT	OCT	NOV	DEC	JAN	FEB	MAR	APR	MAY	JUNE	JULY
1												
2												
3												
4												
5												
6												
7												
8												
9												
10												
11												
12												
13												
14												
15												
16												
17												
18												
19												
20												
21												
22												
23												
24												
25												
26												
27												
28												
29												
30												
31												

STUDENT ATTENDANCE TRACKER

NAME OF STUDENT: _____

	AUG	SEPT	OCT	NOV	DEC	JAN	FEB	MAR	APR	MAY	JUNE	JULY
1												
2												
3												
4												
5												
6												
7												
8												
9												
10												
11												
12												
13												
14												
15												
16												
17												
18												
19												
20												
21												
22												
23												
24												
25												
26												
27												
28												
29												
30												
31												

STUDENT ATTENDANCE TRACKER

NAME OF STUDENT: _____

	AUG	SEPT	OCT	NOV	DEC	JAN	FEB	MAR	APR	MAY	JUNE	JULY
1												
2												
3												
4												
5												
6												
7												
8												
9												
10												
11												
12												
13												
14												
15												
16												
17												
18												
19												
20												
21												
22												
23												
24												
25												
26												
27												
28												
29												
30												
31												

STUDENT ATTENDANCE TRACKER

NAME OF STUDENT: _____

	AUG	SEPT	OCT	NOV	DEC	JAN	FEB	MAR	APR	MAY	JUNE	JULY
1												
2												
3												
4												
5												
6												
7												
8												
9												
10												
11												
12												
13												
14												
15												
16												
17												
18												
19												
20												
21												
22												
23												
24												
25												
26												
27												
28												
29												
30												
31												

STUDENT ATTENDANCE TRACKER

NAME OF STUDENT: _____

	AUG	SEPT	OCT	NOV	DEC	JAN	FEB	MAR	APR	MAY	JUNE	JULY
1												
2												
3												
4												
5												
6												
7												
8												
9												
10												
11												
12												
13												
14												
15												
16												
17												
18												
19												
20												
21												
22												
23												
24												
25												
26												
27												
28												
29												
30												
31												

STUDENT ATTENDANCE TRACKER

NAME OF STUDENT: _____

	AUG	SEPT	OCT	NOV	DEC	JAN	FEB	MAR	APR	MAY	JUNE	JULY
1												
2												
3												
4												
5												
6												
7												
8												
9												
10												
11												
12												
13												
14												
15												
16												
17												
18												
19												
20												
21												
22												
23												
24												
25												
26												
27												
28												
29												
30												
31												

STUDENT ATTENDANCE TRACKER

NAME OF STUDENT: _____

	AUG	SEPT	OCT	NOV	DEC	JAN	FEB	MAR	APR	MAY	JUNE	JULY
1												
2												
3												
4												
5												
6												
7												
8												
9												
10												
11												
12												
13												
14												
15												
16												
17												
18												
19												
20												
21												
22												
23												
24												
25												
26												
27												
28												
29												
30												
31												

STUDENT ATTENDANCE TRACKER

NAME OF STUDENT: _____

	AUG	SEPT	OCT	NOV	DEC	JAN	FEB	MAR	APR	MAY	JUNE	JULY
1												
2												
3												
4												
5												
6												
7												
8												
9												
10												
11												
12												
13												
14												
15												
16												
17												
18												
19												
20												
21												
22												
23												
24												
25												
26												
27												
28												
29												
30												
31												

STUDENT ATTENDANCE TRACKER

NAME OF STUDENT: _____

	AUG	SEPT	OCT	NOV	DEC	JAN	FEB	MAR	APR	MAY	JUNE	JULY
1												
2												
3												
4												
5												
6												
7												
8												
9												
10												
11												
12												
13												
14												
15												
16												
17												
18												
19												
20												
21												
22												
23												
24												
25												
26												
27												
28												
29												
30												
31												

REPORT CARD

NAME OF STUDENT: _____

NAME OF STUDENT	
ADDRESS	
CONTACT NUMBER	
QUARTER / YEAR	
DATE COVERED	

SUBJECT	GRADE	REMARKS

TEACHER'S SIGNATURE:	
PARENT'S SIGNATURE:	

REPORT CARD

NAME OF STUDENT: _____

NAME OF STUDENT	
ADDRESS	
CONTACT NUMBER	
QUARTER / YEAR	
DATE COVERED	

SUBJECT	GRADE	REMARKS

TEACHER'S SIGNATURE:	
PARENT'S SIGNATURE:	

REPORT CARD

NAME OF STUDENT: _____

NAME OF STUDENT	
ADDRESS	
CONTACT NUMBER	
QUARTER / YEAR	
DATE COVERED	

SUBJECT	GRADE	REMARKS

TEACHER'S SIGNATURE: _____

PARENT'S SIGNATURE: _____

REPORT CARD

NAME OF STUDENT: _____

NAME OF STUDENT	
ADDRESS	
CONTACT NUMBER	
QUARTER / YEAR	
DATE COVERED	

SUBJECT	GRADE	REMARKS

TEACHER'S SIGNATURE:	
PARENT'S SIGNATURE:	

REPORT CARD

NAME OF STUDENT: _____

NAME OF STUDENT	
ADDRESS	
CONTACT NUMBER	
QUARTER / YEAR	
DATE COVERED	

SUBJECT	GRADE	REMARKS

TEACHER'S SIGNATURE:	
PARENT'S SIGNATURE:	

REPORT CARD

NAME OF STUDENT: _____

NAME OF STUDENT	
ADDRESS	
CONTACT NUMBER	
QUARTER / YEAR	
DATE COVERED	

SUBJECT	GRADE	REMARKS

TEACHER'S SIGNATURE:	
PARENT'S SIGNATURE:	

REPORT CARD

NAME OF STUDENT: _____

NAME OF STUDENT	
ADDRESS	
CONTACT NUMBER	
QUARTER / YEAR	
DATE COVERED	

SUBJECT	GRADE	REMARKS

TEACHER'S SIGNATURE:	
PARENT'S SIGNATURE:	

REPORT CARD

NAME OF STUDENT: _____

NAME OF STUDENT	
ADDRESS	
CONTACT NUMBER	
QUARTER / YEAR	
DATE COVERED	

SUBJECT	GRADE	REMARKS

TEACHER'S SIGNATURE:	
PARENT'S SIGNATURE:	

REPORT CARD

NAME OF STUDENT: _____

NAME OF STUDENT	
ADDRESS	
CONTACT NUMBER	
QUARTER / YEAR	
DATE COVERED	

SUBJECT	GRADE	REMARKS

TEACHER'S SIGNATURE:	
PARENT'S SIGNATURE:	

REPORT CARD

NAME OF STUDENT: _____

NAME OF STUDENT	
ADDRESS	
CONTACT NUMBER	
QUARTER / YEAR	
DATE COVERED	

SUBJECT	GRADE	REMARKS

TEACHER'S SIGNATURE:	
PARENT'S SIGNATURE:	

REPORT CARD

NAME OF STUDENT: _____

NAME OF STUDENT	
ADDRESS	
CONTACT NUMBER	
QUARTER / YEAR	
DATE COVERED	

SUBJECT	GRADE	REMARKS

TEACHER'S SIGNATURE:	
PARENT'S SIGNATURE:	

REPORT CARD

NAME OF STUDENT: _____

NAME OF STUDENT	
ADDRESS	
CONTACT NUMBER	
QUARTER / YEAR	
DATE COVERED	

SUBJECT	GRADE	REMARKS

TEACHER'S SIGNATURE:	
PARENT'S SIGNATURE:	

REPORT CARD

NAME OF STUDENT: _____

NAME OF STUDENT	
ADDRESS	
CONTACT NUMBER	
QUARTER / YEAR	
DATE COVERED	

SUBJECT	GRADE	REMARKS

TEACHER'S SIGNATURE:	
PARENT'S SIGNATURE:	

REPORT CARD

NAME OF STUDENT: _____

NAME OF STUDENT	
ADDRESS	
CONTACT NUMBER	
QUARTER / YEAR	
DATE COVERED	

SUBJECT	GRADE	REMARKS

TEACHER'S SIGNATURE:	
PARENT'S SIGNATURE:	

REPORT CARD

NAME OF STUDENT: _____

NAME OF STUDENT	
ADDRESS	
CONTACT NUMBER	
QUARTER / YEAR	
DATE COVERED	

SUBJECT	GRADE	REMARKS

TEACHER'S SIGNATURE:	
PARENT'S SIGNATURE:	

REPORT CARD

NAME OF STUDENT: _____

NAME OF STUDENT	
ADDRESS	
CONTACT NUMBER	
QUARTER / YEAR	
DATE COVERED	

SUBJECT	GRADE	REMARKS

TEACHER'S SIGNATURE:	
PARENT'S SIGNATURE:	

REPORT CARD

NAME OF STUDENT: _____

NAME OF STUDENT	
ADDRESS	
CONTACT NUMBER	
QUARTER / YEAR	
DATE COVERED	

SUBJECT	GRADE	REMARKS

TEACHER'S SIGNATURE:	
PARENT'S SIGNATURE:	

REPORT CARD

NAME OF STUDENT: _____

NAME OF STUDENT	
ADDRESS	
CONTACT NUMBER	
QUARTER / YEAR	
DATE COVERED	

SUBJECT	GRADE	REMARKS

TEACHER'S SIGNATURE:	
PARENT'S SIGNATURE:	

REPORT CARD

NAME OF STUDENT: _____

NAME OF STUDENT	
ADDRESS	
CONTACT NUMBER	
QUARTER / YEAR	
DATE COVERED	

SUBJECT	GRADE	REMARKS

TEACHER'S SIGNATURE:	
PARENT'S SIGNATURE:	

REPORT CARD

NAME OF STUDENT: _____

NAME OF STUDENT	
ADDRESS	
CONTACT NUMBER	
QUARTER / YEAR	
DATE COVERED	

SUBJECT	GRADE	REMARKS

TEACHER'S SIGNATURE:	
PARENT'S SIGNATURE:	

REPORT CARD

NAME OF STUDENT: _____

NAME OF STUDENT	
ADDRESS	
CONTACT NUMBER	
QUARTER / YEAR	
DATE COVERED	

SUBJECT	GRADE	REMARKS

TEACHER'S SIGNATURE:	
PARENT'S SIGNATURE:	

REPORT CARD

NAME OF STUDENT: _____

NAME OF STUDENT	
ADDRESS	
CONTACT NUMBER	
QUARTER / YEAR	
DATE COVERED	

SUBJECT	GRADE	REMARKS

TEACHER'S SIGNATURE:	
PARENT'S SIGNATURE:	

REPORT CARD

NAME OF STUDENT: _____

NAME OF STUDENT	
ADDRESS	
CONTACT NUMBER	
QUARTER / YEAR	
DATE COVERED	

SUBJECT	GRADE	REMARKS

TEACHER'S SIGNATURE:	
PARENT'S SIGNATURE:	

REPORT CARD

NAME OF STUDENT: _____

NAME OF STUDENT	
ADDRESS	
CONTACT NUMBER	
QUARTER / YEAR	
DATE COVERED	

SUBJECT	GRADE	REMARKS

TEACHER'S SIGNATURE:	
PARENT'S SIGNATURE:	

REPORT CARD

NAME OF STUDENT: _____

NAME OF STUDENT	
ADDRESS	
CONTACT NUMBER	
QUARTER / YEAR	
DATE COVERED	

SUBJECT	GRADE	REMARKS

TEACHER'S SIGNATURE:	
PARENT'S SIGNATURE:	

REPORT CARD

NAME OF STUDENT: _____

NAME OF STUDENT	
ADDRESS	
CONTACT NUMBER	
QUARTER / YEAR	
DATE COVERED	

SUBJECT	GRADE	REMARKS

TEACHER'S SIGNATURE:	
PARENT'S SIGNATURE:	

REPORT CARD

NAME OF STUDENT: _____

NAME OF STUDENT	
ADDRESS	
CONTACT NUMBER	
QUARTER / YEAR	
DATE COVERED	

SUBJECT	GRADE	REMARKS

TEACHER'S SIGNATURE:	
PARENT'S SIGNATURE:	

REPORT CARD

NAME OF STUDENT: _____

NAME OF STUDENT	
ADDRESS	
CONTACT NUMBER	
QUARTER / YEAR	
DATE COVERED	

SUBJECT	GRADE	REMARKS

TEACHER'S SIGNATURE:	
PARENT'S SIGNATURE:	

REPORT CARD

NAME OF STUDENT: _____

NAME OF STUDENT	
ADDRESS	
CONTACT NUMBER	
QUARTER / YEAR	
DATE COVERED	

SUBJECT	GRADE	REMARKS

TEACHER'S SIGNATURE:	
PARENT'S SIGNATURE:	

REPORT CARD

NAME OF STUDENT: _____

NAME OF STUDENT	
ADDRESS	
CONTACT NUMBER	
QUARTER / YEAR	
DATE COVERED	

SUBJECT	GRADE	REMARKS

TEACHER'S SIGNATURE:	
PARENT'S SIGNATURE:	

REPORT CARD

NAME OF STUDENT: _____

NAME OF STUDENT	
ADDRESS	
CONTACT NUMBER	
QUARTER / YEAR	
DATE COVERED	

SUBJECT	GRADE	REMARKS

TEACHER'S SIGNATURE:	
PARENT'S SIGNATURE:	

REPORT CARD

NAME OF STUDENT: _____

NAME OF STUDENT	
ADDRESS	
CONTACT NUMBER	
QUARTER / YEAR	
DATE COVERED	

SUBJECT	GRADE	REMARKS

TEACHER'S SIGNATURE:	
PARENT'S SIGNATURE:	

REPORT CARD

NAME OF STUDENT: _____

NAME OF STUDENT	
ADDRESS	
CONTACT NUMBER	
QUARTER / YEAR	
DATE COVERED	

SUBJECT	GRADE	REMARKS

TEACHER'S SIGNATURE:	
PARENT'S SIGNATURE:	

REPORT CARD

NAME OF STUDENT: _____

NAME OF STUDENT	
ADDRESS	
CONTACT NUMBER	
QUARTER / YEAR	
DATE COVERED	

SUBJECT	GRADE	REMARKS

TEACHER'S SIGNATURE:	
PARENT'S SIGNATURE:	

REPORT CARD

NAME OF STUDENT: _____

NAME OF STUDENT	
ADDRESS	
CONTACT NUMBER	
QUARTER / YEAR	
DATE COVERED	

SUBJECT	GRADE	REMARKS

TEACHER'S SIGNATURE:	
PARENT'S SIGNATURE:	

REPORT CARD

NAME OF STUDENT: _____

NAME OF STUDENT	
ADDRESS	
CONTACT NUMBER	
QUARTER / YEAR	
DATE COVERED	

SUBJECT	GRADE	REMARKS

TEACHER'S SIGNATURE:	
PARENT'S SIGNATURE:	

REPORT CARD

NAME OF STUDENT: _____

NAME OF STUDENT	
ADDRESS	
CONTACT NUMBER	
QUARTER / YEAR	
DATE COVERED	

SUBJECT	GRADE	REMARKS

TEACHER'S SIGNATURE:	
PARENT'S SIGNATURE:	

REPORT CARD

NAME OF STUDENT: _____

NAME OF STUDENT	
ADDRESS	
CONTACT NUMBER	
QUARTER / YEAR	
DATE COVERED	

SUBJECT	GRADE	REMARKS

TEACHER'S SIGNATURE:	
PARENT'S SIGNATURE:	

REPORT CARD

NAME OF STUDENT: _____

NAME OF STUDENT	
ADDRESS	
CONTACT NUMBER	
QUARTER / YEAR	
DATE COVERED	

SUBJECT	GRADE	REMARKS

TEACHER'S SIGNATURE:	
PARENT'S SIGNATURE:	

REPORT CARD

NAME OF STUDENT: _____

NAME OF STUDENT	
ADDRESS	
CONTACT NUMBER	
QUARTER / YEAR	
DATE COVERED	

SUBJECT	GRADE	REMARKS

TEACHER'S SIGNATURE:	
PARENT'S SIGNATURE:	

We want to thank you for purchasing this book. Our writers and creative team took pride in creating this book, and we have tried to make it as enjoyable as possible.

We would love to hear from you, kindly leave a review if you enjoyed this book so we can do more. Your reviews on our books are highly appreciated. Also, if you have any comments or suggestions, you may reach us at
anglinanelson2010@gmail.com

Regards,
Kylie Taylor

Made in the USA
Las Vegas, NV
12 January 2024

84231988R00083